THE TRIP OF A LIFETIME, WHEREVER YOU GO!

GINNY BROOKS

Copyright © 2018 Ginny Brooks.

All rights reserved. No part of this book may be reproduced, stored, or transmitted by any means—whether auditory, graphic, mechanical, or electronic—without written permission of the author, except in the case of brief excerpts used in critical articles and reviews. Unauthorized reproduction of any part of this work is illegal and is punishable by law.

This book is a journal of our trip and the preparations for it. The things I did, I saw, I heard, and I encountered, as reported, are the way I saw them through my eyes and my opinion of how they appeared to me.

ISBN: 978-1-4834-8418-1 (sc)
ISBN: 978-1-4834-8417-4 (e)

Library of Congress Control Number: 2018904433

Because of the dynamic nature of the Internet, any web addresses or links contained in this book may have changed since publication and may no longer be valid. The views expressed in this work are solely those of the author and do not necessarily reflect the views of the publisher, and the publisher hereby disclaims any responsibility for them.

Lulu Publishing Services rev. date: 04/21/2018

This book is dedicated to my wonderful grandson, Andrew Underwood, and his beautiful wife, Chantel. Thank you for inviting us to your wedding and giving us an opportunity to experience the trip of a lifetime. You are such a precious couple, and I love you both so much.

There is a wedding ahead.
I do not fly and cannot go.
What will we do?
I honestly don't know.

Let us take a road trip.
Let's see the sights.
There is a lot of preparation
To make this trip right.

Preparations are in place.
I am giving them to you.
After sharing our trip of a lifetime,
I hope you will take one, too.

Contents

Preparations for Our Journey xix

Day One 1
    Reidsville North Carolina

Day Two 7
    Lebanon, Tennessee

Day Three 11
    Russellville, Arkansas

Day Four 15
    Amarillo, Texas

Day Five 19
    Gallup, New Mexico

Day Six 23
    Flagstaff, Arizona

Day Seven 29
    Flagstaff, Arizona

Day Eight 35
    Las Vegas, Nevada

Day Nine 41
    Barstow, California

Day Ten 47
    Burbank, California

Day Eleven 53
   Arroyo Grande, California
Day Twelve 61
   Carmel, California
Day Thirteen 69
   Rohnert Park, California
Day Fourteen 73
   Redwood Trees
Day Fifteen 77
   Santa Rosa
Day Sixteen 79
   Wedding Rehearsal
Day Seventeen 81
   Wedding
Day Eighteen 85
   San Francisco, California
Day Nineteen 93
   Fairfield, California
Day Twenty 97
   Reno, Nevada
Day Twenty-One 101
   Elko, Nevada
Day Twenty-Two 107
   Logan, Utah
Day Twenty-Three 111
   Jackson Hole, Wyoming

Day Twenty-Four 117
    Cody, Wyoming
Day Twenty-Five 121
    Casper, Wyoming
Day Twenty-Six 125
    Rapid City, South Dakota
Day Twenty-Seven 131
    Mitchell, South Dakota
Day Twenty-Eight 133
    Moline, Illinois
Day Twenty-Nine 135
    Richmond, Indiana

Was It Worth It? 137
Tornado Alley 139
Senior Lifetime Pass Changes 141
Your Notes for Your Trip of a Lifetime 143

Ginny Brooks lives with her husband in north, central North Carolina. She is a financial advisor, who retired from the business she owned for nineteen years to do "whatever she wanted." "Whatever she wanted" is keeping her busier than she has ever been in her life, with things that are so rewarding and so much fun!

A beach bum through and through, she is most relaxed when she is sitting on the porch of her family's beach cottage at North Myrtle Beach, South Carolina, or walking on the beach early in the morning enjoying God's majestic artwork, and looking for shells.

She loves her time spent with the Bible Study Fellowship ladies and all that she continues to learn from their discussions.

After this fantastic trip, she felt like she had to share the ideas she used to save money, the discoveries she found to give her a little more peace of mind while traveling, and the car-packing tips. She also plans to go along with you as a tour guide.

This is her first published, "whatever she wanted" book.

Thank you to my grandson, Tanner Brooks, for using the knowledge he acquired in his college creative writing class to guide me in the right direction. I also thank my wonderful daughter-in-law, Denise Brooks, for using her teacher skills to take me to the next level, among them, the computer technology involved in writing a book. A special thank you to Mollie Rierson for taking all my mistakes, and making them into a readable book. Also, thank you, John Laskey, for returning my phone call and giving me all the correct answers. To my grandson, Adam Underwood, who is a graphic designer, thank you for using your knowledge and skills to perfect the images in the book and on the cover. Last, but not least, I want to thank my sons, Kris Brooks and Jay Brooks, who used their computer intelligence to help their computer illiterate mom set up a new computer and complete all the issues to get a final draft to the publisher. Jay, you have probably memorized this book, by now. I could not have done it without the help from each of you.

A special thank you to my husband, Phil, for sharing this trip of a lifetime with me. The things we did, the places we went, the experiences we had – all these wonderful memories will stay with me forever. Even after twenty-nine days of complete togetherness, I still love you.

Dear Reader,

As you read this book, I hope that you will enjoy reading about the places we visited, the things we experienced, the wedding we attended, and the fun things and not so fun things we encountered along the way.

Although this book will take you from Reidsville, North Carolina, on a southern route to Santa Rosa, California, and on a northern route back to Reidsville, I hope that after reading it, you will be so thirsty to see for yourself how the beautiful scenery in our country continues to change as you move along your route, and how a little planning can reduce the expense quite a bit. You may even decide to jump in from wherever you are located and embark on a journey of your own.

I have tried to put enough information and tips that we used on our trip that will guide you to plan and save on your own trip, whether the destination is Washington State, Florida, Maine or Colorado. The steps for preparation are the same. The tips for saving money are the same, and you will be equipped with the knowledge of what you need to do to prepare and how you can get the most out of the things you see and the way you travel.

Now, either join the route and see for yourself, or plan your own trip to wherever you please with the tips provided. **Don't forget to take the book along as a guide**.

Happy Travels!
Ginny Brooks

Preparations for Our Journey

These are initial preparations and throughout the book, I will explain how some of them are used.

We are members of American Automobile Association (AAA). I call them to inform them we have a destination of Santa Rosa, California, and will be leaving from Reidsville, North Carolina. I would like a route that will take us to the Grand Canyon, Yellowstone, and with as many tourist attractions as possible along the way. We will be going through Tornado Alley during tornado season, and I would like to miss as much of that as possible.

The next step is to determine how many days we need to allow us to get to Santa Rosa and make the reservation for the length of stay there. That is the only reservation we will make before we leave.

We love to stay at Hampton Inns, and they are part of Hilton Honors membership. I called and got set up to become a Hilton Honors member. There are no fees, but there are perks.

We will be carrying two credit cards in case some places do not honor one. I called the credit card companies to tell them of our trip, so when the charges start coming in, they will know they are legitimate. I always like to be prepared in case of an emergency, and I asked them to increase our credit limit for this length of time, and then put it back at the end of our trip. They agreed to do this. One of the companies even gave me a toll-free phone number to carry with us. The gentleman I spoke with said that because of our advance notification, if we encounter any problems with our credit card along the way, they might be able to help us immediately with our problem. I learned if I try to get a cash advance on a credit card, there will be a fee. Some places will let you buy something and add a small amount to the bill for a cash advance, but most will not. However, you can get a cash advance on a debit card with no fee, unless you use an automated teller machine that does not honor that card for free. We have one debit card we use for a specific purpose and only keep a small amount in that account. For the trip, we deposited $1,000.00 there just in case.

The only thing that concerns me is if we get seriously sick, or are involved in an automobile accident on the other side of the country and need to be hospitalized. How can we get the sick one home? What will we do with the car? God always provides. We just received something in the mail from AAA, and they are starting a new program (or new to me) called Emergency Assistance Plus. They help with everything I was concerned about and much more. We now have this protection, and I have my peace of mind.

I believe Benjamin Franklin's statement "a penny saved is

a penny earned." We know this trip will be expensive, and we know there are many ways we can cut these expenses without giving up anything. Normally on a trip, we take a break at a convenience store and leave with something to drink, a pack of crackers, or a candy bar. The bill is always between $5.00 and $7.00. Mid-morning and mid-afternoon breaks together can easily total $10.00 to $15.00 a day. To lower our cost, I went to Sam's Club and bought in bulk the things I thought we would eat plus a few other things to make our lunch free during the day.

We were aware that the National Parks Service has a lifetime pass for U.S citizens who are sixty-two years or older, but we have never purchased one until now. We invested $10.00 each and now can get into most national parks across the country for free.

The final thing we need is one of those clothes racks that hangs above the back seat. I will explain later how this helps in our packing and in handling our clothes situation.

These things are all in place before we begin our trip.

Day One

It is 7:15 am and we are ready to start our trip of a lifetime.

When our grandson, Andrew, first told us he and his fiancé, Chantel were getting married in Santa Rosa, California, we were concerned because I don't fly and we live in Reidsville, North Carolina - all the way across the country. Then Phil and I started talking. Neither of us has been west of the Mississippi, and we have always wanted to see the Grand Canyon. We are retired and can afford to give thirty days of our life to the trip of a lifetime.

We packed the car last night except for last minute things. We have a Honda CRV and decided to use the back for Andrew's golf clubs, which we are taking out to him, as well as food. When I went to Sam's Club, I bought boxes of individually wrapped assorted chips, crackers, cookies, candy bars and suckers. There are a lot of boxes, but we will be gone a long time. I also got jars of peanut butter, small paper plates, plastic cups, and plastic knives, forks, and spoons. I looked for specials on bottled water and individual bottles of diet cola. I took a plastic milk crate and put a roll of paper towels, hand sanitizer, the plates, cups and utensils in there. I filled a gallon-sized Ziploc bag with sandwich bags, and another with quart-sized bags, and another with folded gallon-sized bags. These all went into the milk crate, as well. So now we have a box for the chips, a box for the crackers, a box for each of the things I bought at Sam's Club, plus the milk crate filled with things for a picnic. We are carrying a small hard-covered ice chest that will hold a little more than a six-pack of drinks. Instead of putting in loose ice, which will be messy as the ice melts, we decide to put ice into gallon Ziploc bags. That way, if we want a drink with ice, we have the cups, the drink, and clean ice cubes. We plan to carry the ice chest to the hotel room each night, put any drinks in it into the refrigerator that we always request when we reserve our room, empty the ice in the bags, and refill the bags the next morning to fill the ice chest for the day. The only other thing in the back is a huge, empty laundry bag. Each morning when we leave the hotel, we can put our dirty clothes into the plastic bag the hotel provides. When we get to the car, we will transfer clothes to our laundry bag and dispose of the other one. The back of our CRV is full.

Next, we went to the back seat. We extended the bar for the clothes from side to side, and then put all our clothes on coat hangers on the rack, along with clothes we will wear to the wedding, which are in plastic bags. We each packed our own duffel bags with undies, sleepwear, and, of course, makeup in mine. All shoes are in a separate duffel bag, including dress shoes for the wedding. When we packed, I took a large tote bag and made a medicine bag. I put all cold and headache medicine into one Ziplock plastic bag, all stomach medicine into another, first aid in another, and so forth. If we need anything over-the-counter for any ailment or pain, it is in that bag. We have another tote bag with computers and cameras. Our thinking is that when we stop each night; we will each pick what we want to wear the next day, take those coat hangers only off the rack, and carry our duffel bags, the two tote bags and the ice chest into the hotel. If we want anything to eat that night for a midnight snack, we'll just raid our stash of food in the back and throw it in the tote bag to carry up to our hotel room. It will sure beat carrying a heavy suitcase holding two weeks of clothes each night. Just like the back of the car, the back seat is full as well.

Now we have just put in last-minute things. The lights in the house are off, the door is locked, and we get in the car. The first thing Phil realizes is you cannot see out the back window if clothes are spread all the way across the rack. He gets out and pushes the clothes all the way over so they are directly behind him. Now, he can see.

He gets back in the car, seat belts are on, and we are so excited to begin our trip. He turns the key in the ignition, and nothing happens. He tries several more times. Oh, did I tell you we also packed our portable battery charger and tire inflator to take with us, just in case? He gets out of the car to get it and realizes it is packed in the back under Andrew's golf clubs and behind all the boxes of food and the ice chest. We unpack the back in the driveway, get the charger, crank the car, and repack the back and at last, we pull out of the driveway. I am thinking. I hope this is not an omen of things to come.

We are close enough to home that there are no tourist attractions that we have not seen. We are just making miles today.

We are staying tonight at a Hampton Inn in Lebanon, Tennessee.

Expenses for Day One   Hotel   124.51
                        Food   37.55
                        Gas   24.00
                        Total   186.06

Gas is $2.459 per gallon at a service station one mile from the exit to Danridge, Tennessee, on May 22, 2015.

Day Two

Our second day takes us through Nashville and Memphis, Tennessee. We were planning to do some sightseeing in both cities, but our son, Kris, reminded us that these cities could be a weekend trip from home. He suggested we keep moving west and use the time saved to see more things further away from home that we may not have an opportunity to see again. This is good advice, and we are taking it.

We have never seen the Mississippi River, so we are going to stop and put our feet in the water for pictures to send home. There is a very colorful park for children up the hill from the bank of the river. We walk along the bank for a while and decide it is time to move on.

We are heading to the bridge, and as I look to the right, I see St. Jude Children's Research Hospital. I knew it was in Memphis, but had not remembered, today, until I looked over and saw it. I close my eyes to lift a prayer up for the children and their families who are in that hospital, and to thank God for all the generous people who donate their money and time to help the operations and the medical staff who work there.

As we leave Tennessee and the Mississippi River and enter Arkansas, I notice there is a sign welcoming people to West

Memphis, Arkansas. I never knew Memphis was on both sides of the Mississippi River and in two different states. It is only the second day of our trip, and I have had my first geography lesson. I also observe how flat the land is becoming. It is easy to see why tornadoes build up. There are no hills or mountains to break up a cloud, so it can just keep building.

We are driving through Arkansas, which is a part of tornado alley, and it is tornado season. In recent weeks, the weather has been unsettled, and there have been a lot of tornadoes. So, being a North Carolina girl who has never experienced these monsters, I want to learn as much as possible about how to stay safe in the event of a tornado. We stop at the Arkansas Welcome Center, and I learn a lot. I am given a list of "Road Condition Phone Numbers" for several states in tornado alley. For your convenience, I am listing them here:

Arkansas	800-245-1672
Colorado	303-639-1111
Kansas	866-511-5368
Missouri	800-222-6400
New Mexico	800-432-4269
Oklahoma	888-425-2385
Texas	800-452-9292

They tell me if I see a funnel cloud, to notice the mile marker number on the side of the road and call the phone number for the state I am in, to give them the road I am on including direction (such as I-40-west), and give them the number of the last mile marker I passed. They will then tell me the exit to take (usually the next one) and direct me to a "safe" building. They say that in tornado alley, most businesses are required to have safe rooms and to make them available and open to all. This information makes me feel much more knowledgeable in the event of facing a tornado. I hope it will help you, as well.

The Lord blessed us. There was no severe weather as we traveled through the state, but I will always keep those numbers for any future travel.

We are staying tonight at a Hampton Inn in Russellville, Arkansas.

Expenses for Day Two   Hotel   111.84
                        Food   28.64
                        Gas   23.00
                        Total   163.48

Gas is $2.339 per gallon in Fairview, Tennessee, on May 23, 2015.

Day Three

We are leaving Russellville, Arkansas, knowing we are in for a rough day. From Oklahoma to Texas, there has been rain, rain and more rain, some tornadoes, and a lot of flooding. We are on our way, and it is raining very hard. Just as we reach Oklahoma City, we really hit the hard rain. There is a tractor-trailer truck in front of us. Phil can see his taillights and that is it. Our thinking is, we are on I-40 and that is a major highway so the tractor- trailer more than likely will continue to go the same way we are going. Since we cannot see any road signs, and the only thing we can see are the taillights of that truck, we will follow him. If he is heading to Alaska, so will we.

I cannot help but think of the young man I met last night. He is riding his bicycle from the east coast to the west coast to raise money for little known diseases. It seems that one of his best friend's sister died from a rare disease. He told me that a lot of money could be raised for cancer research, and heart research, because so many people die from them. When someone dies from a disease that only affects 5% of the population, there are not enough people interested in donating money for that specific disease to be able to fund any research. He usually appears on local television stations along his route, with that state's governor, to bring attention to his fundraising efforts. He has an arrival date for the west coast, and that will be televised, as well. Where is he in this rain? There is no way he can ride a bicycle in this, and there is no way he can see where he is going. I hope he is safe and dry, and will still be able to make his arrival on the west coast on time.

 I am also thinking of a couple I met last night, who are driving their motorcycles to Phoenix, Arizona, to a motorcycle convention for veterans. They, too, have a date to be there for opening ceremonies. They appear to be in their sixties. I see no way they can drive their motorcycles in this, and I do not think they can see where they are going. I say a prayer for the safety of all three.

 The heavy rain lasted about two hours. One highway is closed from flooding, and now that we can see further than taillights, there are yards and farms flooded everywhere. Every river we cross is well out of its banks.

 Now that the rain has become an on and off issue, we notice a sign on Hwy. 40 for a Route 66 museum. We need to stop and calm our nerves. This seems like a perfect way to do just that.

 This place is awesome. All I knew about Route 66 was it was a famous highway. I am learning it went from Chicago to California. As we travel further in our trip, we will notice some of the old road still exists, and a lot of the motels, restaurants, and service stations on the old road are still in operation today - each becoming a separate tourist attraction. I also am learning that the new Interstate 40 was built on top of a lot of

Route 66. So, you ride on Route 66 when you are on Hwy 40, but there are a lot of places you can take a turn and step back in time sixty years ago.

After a rough day, we stop at a Hampton Inn in Amarillo, Texas for the night. These employees are so nice. They tell me I can call them while we are travelling, and they will tell us the nearest Hampton Inn and phone number for us to get reservations for each night.

It seems only fitting to have steaks for dinner since we are in cattle country. We see a family-owned restaurant by the name of Hoffbrau Steaks. The outside is in corrugated steel, and there is a silo connected to the front on the left. The door to the silo is the entrance door. The ceiling has old-timey wooden screen doors placed randomly on it. The walls are part corrugated steel roofing panels in different colors just as they came off other buildings and old used boards. Light fixtures are made from wind turbines. Very unique, but a perfect atmosphere for a Texas steak house. Phil asks the waiter what he recommends. He tells him the most popular steak on the menu is one they smoke for hours, then cut, and finish cooking to the doneness requested by the customer. I have never tasted a more flavorful and tender steak in my life. I believe I could have cut it with a butter knife. It is absolutely the best meal so far.

Expenses for Day Three	Hotel	148.35
	Food	58.54
	Gas	66.17
	Total	273.06

Gas is $2.395 per gallon in Russellville, Arkansas on May 24, 2015.

Gas is $2.378 per gallon in Shawnee, Oklahoma on May 24, 2015.

Gas is $2.499 per gallon in Claude, Texas on May 24, 2015.

Day Four

As we start a new day, I am so thankful we got through all the rain and poor visibility yesterday with no accident. Television reports last night said they had gotten five inches of rain yesterday. I am also thankful that we now have the AAA Emergency Assistance Plus coverage. For those of you who travel, if you haven't researched this, you really need to. No, I do not work for AAA, but this coverage is exactly what we need to give us peace of mind should we be involved in a serious accident with injuries, or have health problems requiring hospitalization.

Phil is aware of famous Cadillacs buried nose down somewhere near Amarillo, Texas, but we cannot find any information on their location. We are riding down Hwy. 40 and have already decided that we are not going to find them, and suddenly, there they are. Quite a tourist attraction! They are in a field with a fence around them, but all you do is open the gate and walk right up to them.

The wind is really picking up as we enter New Mexico. We are stopping at a rest stop for lunch, and the picnic tables are enclosed by three-sided adobe shelters with small windows on each end. It would be impossible for anyone to picnic here if it weren't for these shelters because everything would blow away.

This is where I see the first of many signs, warning of the presence of poisonous snakes.

We get out our banana and uneaten bagel from breakfast, pull out our peanut butter and plastic knife to make our peanut and banana bagel, and place it on our paper plate. Then, we pick out the chips to add to our lunch. There is only one problem with the chips. They are in a large box that takes up a lot of room, and if they are not kept in the box, they will get crushed. Although they take up a lot of room, they are worth it. My thinking is that we are continually eating the food in the back and throwing away all the used items. (We will also give Andrew his golf clubs when we get to Santa Rosa, which will free up space.) With a reduction of items in the back, there is room for the souvenirs we purchase along the way.

After finishing our lunch, we choose a cookie for dessert, refill our drinks and continue our trip.

There are no tourist stops for the afternoon and we are just making mileage, but the change in scenery is becoming more evident the further we go.

We are staying tonight at a Hampton Inn in Gallup, New Mexico.

Cadillacs buried nose down near Amarillo, Texas

Expenses for Day Four	Hotel	148.10
	Food	32.17
	Gas	32.01
	Total	212.28

Gas is $2.999 per gallon in Clines Corner, New Mexico on May 25, 2015.

Day Five

We are leaving Gallup, New Mexico, heading west. The scenery is really changing. The flat plains are slowly becoming sprinkled with mountains, and each scene is prettier than the one before.

Our friends back home are texting and calling to see if we are all right. Record-breaking rains are leaving many of the towns we have been through with a lot of flooding. We are blessed that we have been able to safely travel and continue our trip.

We are heading to the Grand Canyon when we see a sign "Petrified Forest National Park and the Painted Desert," with an arrow pointing to the right. I point to the sign and tell Phil I have always heard of it, but never knew where it was. He said the same thing and took a sharp right. We are now heading in that direction. It's our trip, our decisions, and we want to see this.

Although the Petrified Forest National Park was established in 1906, the fractured segments of the petrified wood lying on the surface of eroding badlands were buried intact some 225 million years ago. Over time, the logs fractured and broke into segments prior to exposure. This is one of the world's largest and most colorful deposits of petrified wood.

The Painted Desert is sometimes mistakenly thought of as a separate park, but it is a geologic formation arching from Petrified Forest National Park to the eastern edge of the Grand Canyon. The fossil record contained in the geologic layer is called the "Chinle Formation." This colorful sediment is also known as the Painted Desert.

We can drive our car through the 28-mile journey through the park and stop at the many overlooks throughout the park to take pictures. I have my cell phone to take pictures to text home to family and friends. I also have my camera for zooming in and videos. Phil has his camera to use for zooming in and videos, and his tablet, which takes the best pictures of all. The scenery is so beautiful. We are stopping at every overlook - every scene is different from the last.

Now, Phil is a Model T Ford enthusiast. He has two and drives them on tours with the two clubs, of which he is a member. He can spot an antique car from a mile away. We are driving along this 28-mile trip through Petrified Forest National Park, stopping at all overlooks, and taking pictures of the beautiful scenery. Suddenly, he slams on the brakes, stops and jumps out of the car with his camera. I am looking around for the spectacular view, and there he is, taking a picture of an old, rusted (I don't know what year) Studebaker. In the front of the car, there is a small brick wall that has been constructed with the chrome grill of a late '50s Cadillac embedded. Of course, I get out and get a picture of him and the car. I know his friend, Craig, and our sons Kris and Jay will understand. So, I text them, "Would you believe, in the middle of the Petrified National Forest, Phil has found an old car?" They text back, "If there is one around, he will find it."

We had already paid $10.00 each to get Senior Lifetime Passes to National Parks. Admission to this park is $10.00 a car. After just $10.00 more in admission fees, we will begin saving on all future admissions. The good thing about this Senior Lifetime Pass is it is good for everyone in a car if the admission fee is per car. If the admission fee is per person, each pass is good for the pass holder and three persons (age 16 and older). When we got our pass, we went to Guilford Courthouse National Military Park in Greensboro, North Carolina. We understand you can purchase these at any national park.

We are eating tonight at a place called Smashburger. They have a special sauce for the burgers and fries. It tastes like olive oil, garlic and something else. It is very good and a really nice change to the regular burger and fries. Evidently, the locals like it, too, because they are very busy.

We are staying tonight at a Hampton Inn in Flagstaff, Arizona.

Expenses for Day Five   Hotel   146.51
                                   Food   21.35
                                   Gas   30.00
                                   Total   197.86

Gas is $3.00 per gallon in Petrified Forest, Arizona on May 26, 2015.

Day Six

What a wonderful way to celebrate our fifty-third wedding anniversary. When we left home, Phil told our friend, Scott, to be on call to come and get me, because he felt like 25 miles of my backseat driving would be about all he could handle. Well, we have made it to day 6 and I am still in the car, so evidently, after fifty-three years, I have trained him to listen to my words of wisdom, or he has learned to turn them off completely. Either way, we are heading to the Grand Canyon.

Admission to the Grand Canyon is $25.00 a car. Since we only need to spend $10.00 more to break even on the cost of our Senior Lifetime Passes, we have now done that, and are beginning to realize a savings of $15.00 at this point. I can live with this. Saving money is making money.

Our admission includes a bus tour with many scenic overlooks along the way. We have our choice to get off the bus at every stop, take as many pictures as we like, and get back on the next bus that comes by (usually no more than a five-minute wait), or we can stay on the bus and only get off at the scenic overlooks that really impress us. The thing is - they all impress us. My first impression is...overwhelming. It is vast. Awesome. I am breathless. It is God's masterpiece. The canyon is 277 river miles long, up to 18 miles wide, and a mile deep. Now that is a big hole!

Phil and I are prepared. I have my cell phone for texting pictures to family and friends fully charged, and the battery for my camera for zooming in and videos is fully charged. I am ready for the day. Phil has his camera and tablet fully charged and he, too, is ready for the day. We are stopping at every stop, and every view is as breathtaking as the last - click, click, click go our cameras because there is no way to describe the Grand Canyon on paper. We know the pictures are the only way we can share these views with our friends. We are at two stops before the end of the bus tour when my cell phone flashes "battery low." I guess a full day of constantly taking pictures will do that to a cell phone. After a few more "I've just got to text a picture of this" shots, the phone cuts off completely (also showing, "memory full"). Well, at least I still have my camera. As we begin taking pictures at the last stop, my camera flashes "memory full." I run over to Phil to tell him both of my cameras were out of commission when he showed me his camera, which flashed "battery low", and we know what that means. We are leaving the Grand Canyon with one out of four cameras still taking pictures.

Before we leave, I need to get souvenirs. I know that my grandson, Austin, will want something from here. My granddaughter, Savannah, will also want something from here.

It is late, and we have been here all day. We are exhausted. We decide we will be better going back to Flagstaff for the night and backtracking in the morning - besides, we both really want another smashburger.

The Hampton Inn where we stayed last night has no vacancies by the time we get back to Flagstaff tonight. We have learned to decide where we want to stay around 2:00 in the afternoon and call ahead for a reservation. Anytime from 5:30 on is a gamble. We were so wrapped up in the Grand Canyon and using all the memory on all our cameras, that getting a room for tonight was the least of our concern.

We have a room for the night and are heading out to eat. We still have a lot to do before bedtime. We need to transfer all the pictures from everything to our computers so we can start tomorrow with a lot of memory available for more pictures. We do not want to miss anything.

We are staying tonight at a Doubletree Hotel in Flagstaff, Arizona.

The Grand Canyon

THE TRIP OF A LIFETIME, WHEREVER YOU GO!

Expenses for Day Six   Hotel   199.21
Food   21.35
Gas   30.00
Total   250.56

Gas is $3.699 per gallon at Grand Canyon Texaco, Arizona on May 27, 2015.

Day Seven

We are spoiled to Hampton Inn with their free, hot breakfasts. The hotel we stayed at last night did not have the free hot breakfast, and we are now riding around Flagstaff looking for a restaurant.

Phil noticed Galaxy Diner and we are going to give it a try. The decor is typical of the 50's with Route 66 signs, and pictures of movie stars from years past, many autographed. The floor is of black and white squares, and the counter is white trimmed in black and red. The booths and the stool seats are in red. The jukebox along the wall is playing songs that fit right in with the decor. We love it. Not only is the price reasonable, but the food is delicious, and we feel like we have just seen another excellent tourist attraction.

I cannot believe it! Phil has just found another 19 (whatever old) truck in a parking lot. Of course, we will stop so he can take pictures.

We are on our way to Hoover Dam. Hoover Dam was created by blocking the Colorado River to form Lake Mead. The purpose was to provide water and hydroelectric power for the developing southwest.

We have reached our destination. Due to a severe drought,

the Lake Mead water levels are reaching record low levels, but it is still a very impressive sight. First, we are taking a tour of the museum. Strict security? Yes. They are just like an airport security check. As we dump our belongings on a table, and they rumble through it all, they decide that the little pocket knife Phil carries for things like opening something taped tight, has become theirs if we want to continue our museum visit. He could have left it in the car, but we did not even think about the fact that a huge power generating facility furnishing electricity to millions needs to be secure. Thank goodness, they are protecting our country, and we are learning a very valuable lesson. Check your pockets before going in any government facility or power generating facility, and leave everything but cash and car keys in the car. The attendant tells us we can go back to the car, leave the knife, and come back, but Phil says the walk is too far and the knife can be replaced.

We are leaving the museum and walking toward the dam. There is a road going over the dam, that people and cars can both travel on. This road connects the states of Arizona and Nevada. Phil wants to walk over it. I am staying on this side looking at all the power lines constructed around the dam and thinking. *It must be a spectacular light show during a thunderstorm.* Phil returns, and we get in our car and drive across that same road over the dam. We turn left and park in the lot on the left. As we get out of the car, the panoramic view is awesome. We can see the water level mark on the rocks and see how low the water level is from the drought. I can just imagine the view when the lake is full.

There is an impressive arch bridge in view that spans the Colorado River and connects the states of Arizona and Nevada. The concrete arch is designed to support the bridge, and its curved shape spans the gap of Black Canyon. In my research, I learn that the construction of this bridge began in 2005 and was completed in 2010, with a cost of $240 million. The bridge, which is known as the Hoover Dam Bypass, is also known as the Mike O'Callaghan-Pat Tillman Memorial Bridge. We return to our car, leave Nevada, cross over the dam, enter Arizona, to continue our trip.

Before we left home, Phil's mother, Thelma, showed some concern that we would be gone so long on a road trip across the country. To help put her mind at ease, I told her every night when we stop, I will text her daughter, Pat, and her granddaughter, Stacey, and let them know where we are. Our breakfast friends, who eat at the big table at the restaurant, want us to stay in touch, and our friends, Jo and Scott, are to be contact people for that group. In addition, I need to keep our sons, Kris and Jay informed, as well as daughters-in-law Regina and Denise. You know how group texts are. You send it to everyone, and if any of the group texts back, it goes to everyone, which can create havoc. Therefore, I began a tradition that every night after we check into the hotel, I am texting Pat and Stacey, Jo and Scott, and Kris, Jay, Regina and Denise. This means I will send four or more separate texts. I am telling them what we saw each day and where we are staying each night. I am also sending at least two pictures of the highlight of the day. Little did I know that when we returned from our trip, Phil's mother, who is in her nineties, would grab my hand and say, "I don't know how much it cost you to send those pictures each day, but whatever it is, I will pay you for it." "I enjoyed every day of your trip." Because of her response, and the response of the others we texted, I will always make that a part of any future trip of this nature.

Now we are heading for the city of lights, Las Vegas. We are tired and have decided we will check into our hotel, get a bite to eat, and just ride down the strip to see the nightlife, and call it a day.

We are staying tonight at a Hampton Inn in Las Vegas, Nevada.

Expenses for Day Seven Hotel   122.81
                        Food   52.90
                        Gas   55.00
                        Total   230.71

Gas is $2.99 per gallon in Flagstaff, Arizona on May 28, 2015.

Gas is $3.30 per gallon in Las Vegas, Nevada on May 28, 2015.

Day Eight

Today, I will experience my first trip to a casino. After a good night's sleep, I am ready to take on the world. Now, I really do not want to look too inexperienced about this gambling adventure, so I approach a lady, who looks to be in her fifties, sitting behind the counter. I whisper quietly to her, "I really hate to bother you, but this is my first trip to a casino, and I do not know what I need to do to play the slot machines." She looks up at me and smiles. Her smile reminds me of a kindergarten teacher, and the smile she would give to a student who did not know how to do something, but did not want to be humiliated by the others knowing. She gives me the kindergarten teacher smile that says, "I will help you, and this will be our secret." She talks almost in a whisper so the others behind the counter cannot hear her. What a kind lady! So considerate of those less knowledgeable than her. She comes from behind the counter and takes me to one of the machines right in front of her counter. I don't see a sign, but I think there is one somewhere on the machine that says, "For first-time dummies." Anyway, she sits me down and explains how to play the machine for $1.00, $5.00, $10.00 or $20.00. I explain to her my total investment is $20.00, and to make that money last as long as possible, I guess I need to stick with $1.00. She shows me, and then she leaves. Did I hear her giggle as she left? Oh, well.

I guess it is beginner's luck, because I did everything the lady told me, and suddenly, I have a grand total in winnings of $180.00. Okay, I understand this thing now. Let's see what will happen with a couple of $20.00 bets. Not good. Okay, let's try a couple of $10.00 bets. Not good. I am going back to the $1.00 bets that made me the money in the beginning. But just in case things continue to go south, I need a plan before I get carried away and lose it all. When I reach $90.00, I will leave. Phil is coming back to see how I am doing. I just dropped to $90.00 and remark, "I am ready to go." He says, "Just like that?" "Yes," I tell him, "I am down to $90.00, that's it. I'm through." So, I am **not** walking away with millions, but I am walking away with a little more than I came in with. I had a lot of fun, and have a little better knowledge of slot machines.

Now that I am $90.00 richer, we are ready to leave Las Vegas and head west. We wanted to go by Pawn Stars, but cannot find it. After driving for several blocks, we see a line outside a building and realize it is the Pawn Stars building. How about that? Of course, we are going to stop and check it out. There is a man outside the door telling people they are welcome to come in and take pictures of everything but the cashier area. We are now inside and talking with other tourists. We are told one of the stars was there earlier, but he left right before we got there. The place is a lot smaller than what I envisioned from watching the TV show, but it is a fun visit, if for no other reason, than to say we have been there.

We are now heading west and beginning our journey across the Mojave Desert. There are mountains far away in the background, but the desert itself is nothing. No houses, no buildings, no animals, no people, no nothing. It is perfectly flat. There are cacti and scrub grass. The only trees remind me of the Charlie Brown Christmas Tree, not too tall, scraggly, and give absolutely no shade.

Suddenly, we see a strip mall in Primm, Nevada, with a restaurant by the name of The Mad Greek. We are hungry and do not know what lies ahead as far as food is concerned. Greek food really sounds good about now. The clerk recommends a gyro special that is delicious. And of course, no visit to a Greek restaurant would be complete without baklava. This is a stop I would highly recommend.

We are driving down Highway 15 on our way to Barstow, California, and notice in the middle of the desert, there are three towers with ultra-bright lights on them. We are at a loss as to what we are seeing. We just know we have never seen anything like that before. About that time, our son Kris calls to check on us. Now, Kris is one of the smartest people I know. If he doesn't know the answer to something, he will research the subject until he does. I tell him about these lights, and he asks me to text him the pictures we took. In less than ten minutes, my cell phone notifies me of a text message from Kris. Not only is he giving me his source of research, but he is telling me his research indicates this is the Ivanpah Solar Power Facility as seen from Interstate 15. Thank you, Kris, for educating your mom and dad.

We are on our way to Barstow to check into Hampton Inn for the night. As I step out of the car on our arrival, I am sure I am seeing a mirage. Looking straight from in front of the hotel, there is nothing but flat desert as far as the eye can see. When I look to the left, there is a huge Tanger Outlet Sign. I am so excited to know civilization is right at the back door of the hotel. I am texting all my lady friends and telling them it must be a mirage.

The group texting begins:

My daughter-in-law Regina: "There is always time for shopping."

Me: "I did leave Las Vegas with $90.00."

Regina: "And that's more reason for Tanger shopping."

Me: "Works for me."

My daughter-in-law Denise: "Just saw the conversation! Glad you made some shopping money."

Regina: "Sounds like it was meant to be."

Me: "Do I spend now, or wait for Rodeo Drive?"

Regina: "Decisions, decisions (with a smiley face)."

My niece Stacey: "That's what those plastic cards are for."

My friend Trudie does not text, so I need to call her. As she answers, she laughs and tells me our mutual friend, Jo, has already called her to tell her about my text. Final results - I am using extreme willpower and not going shopping.

We are staying tonight at a Hampton Inn in Barstow, California.

Expenses for Day Eight   Hotel   116.49
                           Food   44.96
                           Gas   34.00
                           Total   195.45

Gas is $3.55 per gallon in Barstow, California on May 29, 2015.

Day Nine

Oh, what a beautiful morning! We are in California and heading west to the Pacific Ocean. The scenery is so beautiful. The desert is disappearing, and the mountains are coming into view.

I see so many huge rocks with artwork on them. There is nothing like this back east, and they are so pretty. After picking up a booklet on this, I have learned they are called "Petroglyphs." This comes from two Greek words: petro - which means rock, and glyph - which means carving or engraving. They are pecked or abraded marks that people have purposely made on rocks in the landscape or on boulders, cliff sides and other rock formations. Petroglyphs have been made for thousands of years by Southwestern Native Americans from many different cultures. The bridges and entrances to the bridges have so much of this artwork etched into them. I can't help but go back in time and wonder if there was a story behind each one, and if so, what it was.

We are entering Capistrano Beach, and there is a wall with birds etched into the side. My thoughts are immediately going back to the song, "When the Swallows Come Back to Capistrano."

I cannot wait to put my toes into the Pacific Ocean. We park and immediately head for the beach. As we approach, we are on a hill and look down to the beach. There are flowering bushes along the way. There are surfers, fishing boats, and pleasure boats dotting the water. On the Atlantic coast beaches, I love to pick up seashells as I walk on the beach. Whoa!!! There are no shells. There are only rocks - pretty rocks.

Since I am a beach bum at heart, my goal is to stop at as many beaches as time will allow and walk on the beach to collect shells from each one. So, I have now learned there are no shells here.

Leaving Capistrano Beach, we are going to start north on State Route 1, which takes us up the coast and mostly in view of the ocean as we travel. The scenery is awesome.

The city of Dana is the first time we notice that the houses are built on the sides of the mountain, almost as if they are stacked. It is an interesting concept and a good way for a lot of people to have an ocean view.

We stop at Laguna Beach and Newport Beach. There are very little to no shells, but a lot of different rocks are on the beaches. I am surprised to find colored rocks, not just grey and dull, but pink and other shades of colors. They are so pretty and so different from the Atlantic Coast. I am glad we brought those Ziplock plastic bags. They are perfect for collecting, labeling, and storing our finds.

Huntington Beach is very cold and windy. We are going down steps to get to the beach to see what items we can find here. As cold as it is to us, people are out on the beach. There are more pretty rocks. I just found my first pieces of sea glass - one pink and one green.

I am collecting whatever Mother Nature sees fit to place on the shore, and learning about the differences in each beach as we travel. As we drove along the highway from east to west, I saw the deserts, mountains, different trees, flowers, and landscapes. I noticed a constant change in scenery. Now that we are on the Pacific Coast going north and stopping at the different beaches, I see the same change in what has been placed on the shores by the incoming tides. I am in awe as I think of all the beauty that God created for us to enjoy. No human could create or design the magnitude of beauty placed in front of us.

We are leaving Huntington Beach and notice there are no people on the beaches at this point. There are big boulders in the water, which might be why there are no people in the water.

The closer we get to Los Angeles, the worse the traffic is getting. Other than fighting traffic in Oklahoma City with "no visibility rain," there has not really been any nerve-wracking traffic -- until now. Time for choices. I really want to see Rodeo Drive. We both really do not want to fight this traffic. So, we decide to hang a right, go northeast, and spend the night in Burbank, California. I am sorry to say we will have to fight the LA traffic a little longer, but it does finally get back to more relaxed driving and riding by the time we stop at Burbank for the night.

We are staying tonight at a Hampton Inn in Burbank, California.

Expenses for Day Nine   Hotel   172.20
                         Food   32.61
                         Gas   33.01
                         Total   237.82

Gas is $3.799 per gallon in Burbank, California on May 31, 2015.

Day Ten

Today we leave Burbank and are heading for Rodeo Drive. I have my money and plan to see if they will sell me a bag (as in a bag in which they put your purchases). From what I have always heard of the prices, I feel that will be all I can afford. And wouldn't that be neat? To have a bag with the name of a store in Rodeo Drive displayed. I can hardly wait. I can touch a dress that some rich and famous person will buy. I would love to look at the price tag, but I am assuming there will be no tags displayed. Will I be gutsy enough to ask? I am not sure.

Hollywood is on our way to Rodeo Drive so we will check it out. One of the things I want to see is the HOLLYWOOD wording on the mountain. It is not where we are, and I really want to have more time for Rodeo Drive, so we decide not to look for it. The section we are going through is not glamorous and reminds me of where the struggling actors and actresses might live. We are going to move on, but Oh! There is the Warner Bros. Building. So now that I have seen something to do with the movies, I am ready to move on to my destination of purpose. **Rodeo Drive, here I come!**

We are here!!! It is 9:00 am on Sunday. The stores and the layout are beautiful. The entire area speaks MONEY in a way I can only observe. There are people everywhere with cameras, and I am snapping pictures with my cell phone with the rest of them. As we turn to go into the first store of my adventure, I spot the sign - "Open at 12:00 noon on Sundays." Phil swears he planned this entire trip for this arrival time. At least, the stores have a lot of windows, so we can see the type of merchandise they sell. We have walked the entire area and looked in every window with all the other tourists, but there is so much more to see. We decide our schedule and my pocketbook will be better off if we don't stay for the stores to open. We are going to ride through Beverly Hills on the way out, just to look at some of the beautiful homes.

Now we are heading back to the Pacific Coast. This means driving back through the worst part of our entire trip traffic wise. I am not sure, but I think there are six lanes each way and it is called the Los Angeles Freeway. Everyone is flying and zigzagging between lanes. These people are probably used to it, but to Phil and me, who are used to a more laid-back lifestyle, we both agree this is a scary drive and find it very nerve-wracking. Thank goodness, it is Sunday morning, and not quite as many people are out as yesterday.

We are now back to the coastal highway. Highway 1 coming north from Los Angeles is also known as the Pacific Coast Highway. Little do we know, we are getting ready to experience one of the most breathtaking rides of our life. Every turn brings another scenic surprise. We are mesmerized by the unique differences at each overlook, and believe me, we are stopping at them all (and there are a lot).

Santa Barbara is our next beach stop. There was an oil spill off the coast several weeks ago, and we can still get a faint smell of oil as we approach. Now on the beach, we are picking up more rocks and some driftwood. The difference between Pacific Coast beaches and Atlantic Coast beaches still amazes me. The main thing is the Pacific Coast beaches have little or no shells and a lot of beautiful rocks. The Atlantic Coast beaches have little or no rocks and a lot of different shells.

Santa Barbara is having an arts fair in a little park overlooking the beach. We are enjoying taking a break from driving and looking at all the art.

It has been another full and fun day, and now we are stopping for the night at Arroyo Grande, which is right at Pismo Beach.

After checking into our hotel and having dinner, we are going to check out Pismo Beach. We find a parking lot with beach access and steps going down to the beach - a lot of steps - 121 steps down and 121 steps back up. I counted them. **Wow!!!** Am I out of shape!!! We find a few more rocks to add to our collection, and then attempt to get back up those 121 steps. Both of us are exhausted when we reach the parking lot, and we meet a woman who lives there, so we decide to talk with her about her beach, while we catch our breath. While we are talking, a young lady, probably in her twenties, passes us dressed in a wetsuit heading down those 121 steps to the beach. The lady tells us that this young lady comes out every afternoon after work and swims for about thirty minutes past the breakers and parallel to the coast. She says that sometimes the dolphins swim with her. I asked her about sharks, and she said one time the lady was swimming, and a great white shark was seen in the water. The people on shore kept calling to warn her, but she was too far out to hear them. Then, suddenly, dolphins showed up and completely circled her and swam with her. The shark left, and she and her dolphin friends completed her swim.

The one thing we are noticing about the beaches since we have gotten on the Pacific Coast Highway is you have a flat beach, and immediately, (like the 121 steps) the landscape goes straight up to mountains across the road.

We are staying tonight at a Hampton Inn in Arroyo Grande, California.

Expenses for Day Ten	Hotel	140.11
	Food	51.07
	Gas	41.00
	Total	232.18

Gas is $3.899 per gallon in Pismo Beach, California on June 1, 2015.

Day Eleven

Our first stop for the day is Hearst Castle in San Simeon, California. Hearst Castle's history began in 1865, when George Hearst purchased 40,000 acres of ranch land.

Admission is $25.00 per person. Because of the severe drought in California, they have porta johns (lots of them) in the parking lot, with signs stating that because of the severe drought, all restrooms within the castle are closed. So, it is now or never for the kidneys. After enjoying the luxuries of the porta john, we enter the gift shop located at the foot of the mountain. As we are walking through the door to board the bus that will take us to the top of the mountain, they are taking pictures. They say, "smile" and snap the picture.

We have boarded a bus at the bottom of the mountain and are being transported to the castle at the top. The bus is going around the narrow, curvy roads much faster than I would like, and the higher we go, the steeper it gets, so I close one eye. This way, I can still see a little, but not as much. Well, this is not working. Will we ever get to the top of this mountain? I close both eyes and pray for the safety of us all. Phil is telling me the scenery is beautiful and to open my eyes and enjoy it.

No way! God and I really need the conversation He and I are having at this exact time.

Here we are at the top of the mountain. The castle is beautiful and has a gorgeous view of the countryside below. My knees are beginning to stop shaking from that bus ride, and I am ready to see just how the rich and famous live. The ceilings and artwork are amazing. Our guide tells us a lot about Randolf Hearst and the Hollywood years, which is very interesting. Everything about the castle is money. The indoor swimming pool is unbelievable. It is hard to describe all the different features of the castle and the stories that go with it.

As we are coming back down the mountain, I realize I can look down at the floor of the bus, rather than out the window, and I can keep my eyes open. Why didn't I think of that going up? I guess God just wanted to hear from me. He did.

The pictures they took of us earlier are ready and they are $32.00. Normally, we don't buy pictures like this, but the background is so good, and one picture is in a customized frame of the castle. The package includes one picture in the customized frame and one without a frame. $32.00 is not bad for these wonderful memories. It is a definite must-see and worth spending half a day of your trip taking this tour. Phil says if he is ever within 100 miles of it, he will go again.

Leaving Hearst Castle, we are back on the Pacific Coast Highway with views that are breathtaking and overlooks all along the way.

One overlook that is so educational is the Piedras Blancas

Elephant Seal Rookery. Our grandson, Austin, would love this. Looking down over the cliff, there is a sandy beach and a lot of large boulders on the beach and in the water. All along the beach there are elephant seals lying there making their elephant seal noises, while some are still in shallow water, flopping and making their noises. Ginny, how would you describe the sounds the elephant seals make? I am thinking it is between a bark and a croak. The sign at the overlook states that elephant seals spend most of their lives at sea, but come ashore at different times of the year to give birth, mate, molt, and rest. From March to April, weaned pups come ashore. They spend a couple of months at the rookery developing swimming and diving skills on their own before taking off on their first foraging trip at sea. This nice lady comes up to me and asks if I know what is going on down on the beach. She has a tee shirt on with "Elephant Seal Society," or something like, that monogrammed on the front, and I am ready to learn all about the actions below. According to her, the seals come ashore for the purpose of molting. April - August is molting season. They will come ashore and stay there for 30 days with no food or water. As the skin dries out and the sea breeze blows over them, their old skin will come off. This happens when they are around six weeks of age. They will lose the black coat they were born with, in favor of a silver coat that gradually turns a shade of brown and tan. After thirty days, they will have all the next layer of skin and will go back into the ocean. The ones on the beach look all spotty. The lady tells me that is part of the old skin and part of the new. Wow! What a learning experience about how much God even plans the lives of elephant seals.

Another overlook gives us a beautiful view of people kitesurfing. Awesome!

Now we can see windsurfers at this overlook.

Other overlooks have regular surfers, other sea life, and breathtaking views. The scenery is unbelievable. Big rocks are in the water and on shore. I can see that it would not be safe to swim there, but it is so different from Atlantic Coast beaches that I am used to seeing. It is like another world, and one that I am so blessed to see.

When we were planning our trip, and trying to decide how many days we would need to get to Santa Rosa on the day of our reservation, we wanted to plan days that we would stop at least every two hours to get out and walk around for about ten minutes, and stop for the day around 4:00 every afternoon, and time for the tourist attractions we want to see. The AAA map has us going up central California to get to Santa Rosa. After talking with friends about the Pacific Coast Highway, we knew we wanted to see that, and we just re-adjusted that part of the route to cover our interest. In calculating the mileage and stops, we came up with a figure of how many days we would need to go the way we want to go and see the things we want to see. Then, we added one more day, in case one of us is sick, or we have car trouble. Prayers were answered and we were not sick and did not have car trouble. However, the day spent at Petrified Forest and Painted Desert was a last-minute decision. Thank goodness, we threw in that extra day. There is so much to see in California that we have had to pick and choose some stops to make sure we get to Santa Rosa for our reservation, and, there is no way we will cut Pebble Beach out of this trip.

It has been another full, awesome and fun day.

We are staying tonight at Carmel Mission Inn at Carmel, California.

Piedras Blancas Elephant Seal Rookery

Expenses for Day Eleven Hotel   149.50
                         Food   31.77
                         Gas   25.00
                         Total   206.27

Gas is $3.699 per gallon in Carmel, California on June 2, 2015.

Day Twelve

It is 8:30 and what a beautiful morning to start the day. Pebble Beach Golf Links, here we come. Our son, Jay and our grandson, Tanner are avid golfers, and I do not want to miss a thing. I will be buying souvenirs for them.

We take the road to Pebble Beach, and there is a ticket booth. We are told it is $10.00 a car to take the 17-Mile Drive. I have never heard of the 17-Mile Drive, but we do not want to miss out on anything. We pay our $10.00 and are on our way through these 17 miles. Wow! The folder they gave us when we gave them our money is impressive. According to the folder, there are twenty-one points of interest on this drive. There are also several more golf courses here. Poppy Hills Golf Course is the home of the Northern California Golf Association. The Inn and Links at Spanish Bay was built in 1987 by Pebble Beach Company. The world- famous resort and golf course are famous for the bagpiper that closes the course each evening. Bird Rock Course has no marker, but at one time, this was the site of the once popular equestrian hunt and steeplechase competitions. It was also used in the 1920s by the 11th Calvary for riding and saber practice. It is now part of the Shore Course of the Monterey Peninsula

Country Club. Spyglass Hill Golf Course is a public golf course designed by Robert Trent Jones, Sr. that takes its theme from the classic tale of Treasure Island. The Lodge at Pebble Beach was built in 1919 and is the heart of Pebble Beach and the home of the world-famous Pebble Beach Golf Links. Open to the public, it offers a variety of dining and shopping options. From the Lodge, one can enjoy the views of the sweeping 18th fairway and green. The Peter Hay Par 3 Golf Course has a monument for the 100th U. S. Open. There is also the Pebble Beach Equestrian Center.

There are several historical points of interest along the drive. Spanish Bay is where Don Gasper de Portola, the Spanish explorer and his group camped in 1769 while searching for Monterey Bay. Point Joe is the place where early mariners often crashed on the rocks after mistakenly setting their course for this point, believing that it was the entrance to Monterey Bay. China Rock and Point Joe are both places that Chinese fishermen built lean tos against the rocks for their homes in the late 1800s and early 1900s.

And how could they not have scenic points of interest! Shepherd's Knoll gives a magnificent view of Monterey Bay and the Santa Cruz Mountains. The Restless Sea is a unique turbulence generated by the submerged terrain off Point Joe. Bird Rock is home to shorebirds and groups of harbor seals and sea lions. The Ghost Tree has a trunk that is bleached white from wind. It is said this unusual Monterey cypress has a sinister silhouette. The Lone Cypress is one of California's most endearing landmarks. It has prevailed on its rocky perch for more than 250 years. This icon is the living symbol of Pebble Beach Company.

We are now entering the parking lot for the Pebble Beach Golf Links. The putting green makes up the center of the facility with buildings around it. On one side, there is a strip with different shops and the pro shop at the end. The Lodge is on the other side of the putting green.

We are here, and I am heading for the pro shop. Need to get those souvenirs. I am trying to decide which ball marker I want to get, when this nice young man comes up and asks if he can help me. I tell him that I have a son who is an avid golfer and a grandson who is playing golf at college and need to get them some things from Pebble Beach. Evidently, my southern accent is giving me away, because he is asking me where I am from. I tell him I am from Reidsville, North Carolina, and he has probably never heard of it, but it is between Greensboro, North Carolina, and Danville, Virginia. The biggest smile is coming on his face as he tells me he is from Danville, Virginia. He asks where my grandson is going to college. Again, I tell him it is a small college, and he has probably never heard of it. Here comes that smile again. It seems he went to my grandson's rival college and played them many times in golf. What a small world in which we live. After two ball markers, two golf hats, one golf ball for each of the men in the family and the women who play golf, and some other things I got because my Danville friend told me Jay and Tanner would like them (of course everything had Pebble Beach Golf on them), I sign my credit card over to them and leave the pro shop.

Phil and I are going over to check out The Lodge. He is going straight back to the room overlooking the 18th fairway and green. He says he thinks this is where the television sports commentators broadcast from when there is a tournament. He walks through the room that is full of tables where people are sitting and eating, and is walking out on the huge balcony. He can watch the golfers as they play the last hole.

I walk down the halls that are filled with trophies and pictures of past tournaments, a history lesson in the making. Some employees are in the room leading out, so I stop and tell them about trying to get as much information as possible for Jay and Tanner. One of the men tells me to come with him. He goes to his computer, punches a few buttons and shows me a screen with a live cam of the putting green on display. He tells me to watch the screen, and he leaves. As I watch the screen, he appears on the edge of the putting green and waves to me. He returns and asks me if I can reach either one of them by phone right now. Jay texted me about an hour ago during a layover on their flight to San Francisco, and I am pretty sure he is back in the air, but I will try to get him---no answer. Tanner is probably in class, but I will try to get him--no answer. My friend says if they had brought up the Pebble Beach website, I could go out to the putting green, stand near the clock, look at the camera, which he would show me the location, and I could wave to them on the live webcam. That would have been so neat. I am sorry that did not work out. Later, in looking back, I wish I had called our friend, Bob. He would have loved to tell his golfing buddies that someone just waved to him from the putting green at Pebble Beach. Sorry about that, Bob.

I think we have really gotten our $10.00 worth from this 17-Mile Drive, and I think Jay and Tanner, and the others, will be pleased with their souvenirs, but it is time to head on up the coast.

As we leave and get back on the Pacific Coast Highway, there is another overlook on Monterey Bay. The ocean and sky are packed with kite surfers. All the many different colored kites are really a sight to behold.

Our original plan was to stop in San Francisco on the way up and do our sightseeing before going to Rohnert Park, which is where we will be staying for the wedding activities. Our reservation begins today. By the time we arrive in San Francisco, we will not have enough time for sightseeing. Thanks to our flexible schedule, we will catch it as we leave.

It is around 5:30 and we pull into our hotel parking lot. When we were planning our trip, we planned what we thought would give us enough time for driving at a relaxing pace, seeing the tourist attractions we wanted to see, and then threw in an extra day, in case one of us had a sick day, or we had car trouble. The only reservation we made before we left home was this reservation for the wedding festivities. We were not sick and did not have car trouble, and we are arriving at 5:30 in the afternoon of our reservation. How is that for timing? We are getting our luggage out of the car when my cell phone rings. It is Jay. He and Denise have just landed in San Francisco and gotten their rental car. They will be driving right past our hotel on their way to Santa Rosa. We are all exhausted, but they are going to stop for a quick hug. So good to see them, even if it is just for a few minutes.

Black Bear Diner, a restaurant just a few blocks from our hotel looks like a nice place, so we are going there for dinner tonight. The food is very good, and the atmosphere is relaxing. When I place my order, and ask for sweet tea, the waitress looks at me and grins. "Where are you from?" she asks. I tell her North Carolina. She informs me that sweet tea is popular in the south, where I am from, but in California, they do not have sweet tea. However, she informs me they have a raspberry tea that she thinks I would like. I have just been introduced to raspberry tea, and I love it. It will be my favorite drink until I get back to sweet tea territory.

We are staying the next several days at a Hampton Inn in Rohnert Park, California.

Windsurfers and Kite Surfers North of Pebble Beach

Expenses for Day Twelve	Hotel	237.38	
	Food	49.65	
	Total		287.03

Day Thirteen

We will be here for five days for a little rest and relaxation and for Andrew and Chantel's wedding festivities. We are staying in Rohnert Park, which is about twelve miles south of Santa Rosa. Santa Rosa is part of Sonoma County Wine Country and quite busy. We want to kick back a little bit and relax more, so we feel like the twelve-mile drive is worth the extra peace and quiet.

First things first. I need to wash clothes and repack for the return trip home. Thank goodness for coin operated washers and dryers in our hotel. I am washing everything we wore on our trip out, and plan to wash what we wear here before we leave, so we will leave with all clean clothes again.

We are riding around Rohnert Park to see what is near us. There are restaurants, a COSTCO and a casino. All right, I did win $90.00 in Las Vegas, so I am a seasoned gambler now. We are going into the casino with my $20.00 gambling money. This is going to be my big win. I am very confident. I do not need to ask questions this time. I know it all. I sit down, insert my $20.00 investment, punch the buttons, and in less than five minutes, they had it all. That just goes to show, you can lose it as quickly (actually quicker) than you can win it. If I stop now,

I will still have a total gambling winning of $70.00. It sounds good to me. I now have the experience of casino gambling. Been there, done that, and do not need to do it again.

Denise is working on wedding things, so Jay is picking us up to take us to some local attractions.

He is taking us through Sebastopol, a beautiful scenic countryside of orchards, vineyards, and redwoods. We are on our way to the Christian camp where Andrew and Chantel work. Andrew, Chantel, Jay, Denise, Phil, and I met at the camp and are eating lunch with the children. It is a very noisy and happy group of campers. You can tell they are thoroughly enjoying their time here.

After visiting with them for a while and seeing the house where Andrew and Chantel will be living, Jay takes us to Monte Rio, and we see the Russian River for the first time. We drive on the road that follows the river to the ocean until we reach Goat Rock State Park, and we can see where the Russian River empties into the Pacific. There are big boulders in the water and on shore. There is a sign there that gets my attention: "**Danger – This is One of the Most Deadly Beaches in California**." Across the road is another sign, "<u>**Tsunami Hazard Zone**</u>." Right above that sign is a **"No Dogs Allowed"** sign. Why do I feel like I am ready to leave this exact section of the coast?

Although Goat Rock State Park is in Bodega Bay, we are now going to the small town of Bodega Bay where a large amount of Alfred Hitchcock's movie, "The Birds" was filmed.

There is a life-sized statue of Alfred Hitchcock in front of one of the stores. Of course, we are going to take a picture of us, with our arm around his shoulder.

Tonight, we get to meet Andrew`s future in-laws, Richard and Janelle. We are going out to dinner with Andrew, Chantel, Richard, Janelle, Jay and Denise. While having a delicious dinner at an Outback Steakhouse, we are given the opportunity to see why Chantel is the precious person she is. Her parents are my kind of people - the type who make you feel as though you have known them forever. What a wonderful night of connecting. It also gives me a great sense of peace, knowing that although Andrew is living on the other side of the country, he will have a family of this caliber close to him should he need them. It has been a very relaxing and enjoyable night.

Day Fourteen

Another day dawns, another adventure awaits. We are meeting for lunch with Jay, Denise, Andrew, and Chantel at Ike's in Santa Rosa. They are famous for their subs, and now, I know why. They are fantastic. It is a beautiful day, and we are eating outside. Perfect.

Now that we have had lunch, Andrew and Chantel are giving us a tour of The Big Basin Redwoods State Park at Wadell Beach. One of the trees is named Parson Jones. The sign states Height - 310 feet, Diameter - 13.8 feet, Approximate age - 1300 years. Another tree is named Colonel Armstrong. The sign states Height - 308 feet, Diameter - 14.6 feet, Approximate age - 1400 years. The root system as seen on top of the ground is almost as impressive as the height, diameter, and age.

We are now back at the camp, and Andrew is taking us on a tour here. We are riding through the camp on something like a four-wheeler, but a little bigger. There are children everywhere doing different things. The ones at the rock-climbing wall are shouting to Andrew for him to watch them. No matter where we go, they call to Andrew, and he shouts back to them.

Andrew gives us a very interesting lesson on redwood trees. The thing that stuck with me the most is how God protects these trees. They are very drought resistant, and California is in a very serious drought that has been going on for many years. He shows us damage done to the trees from lightning strikes, and then shows us where new little trees are sprouting at the base. It is almost like Mother Nature is saying, "Just in case this tree does not survive, I will give it an offspring to keep the tree alive for generations to come."

We are going to Andrew and Chantel's home. They are fortunate to be able to rent one of the houses on the grounds of the camp. It is perfect for the newlyweds, and they are right there at work. They are still moving in, but it is already evident that Chantel is turning it into a comfortable and inviting home.

Tripp arrives from Reidsville amid much laughter, shouting, and hugs. He and Andrew have been best friends since childhood, and he is going to be a groomsman in the wedding. After he comes in their house, we get our hugs, say hello, thank Andrew and Chantel for a wonderful day, and leave the young people to continue their reunion.

We noticed a neat little fast food place near our hotel by the name of In & Out Burger. Richard told us that it was very good. We are tired, so we think we will try it tonight. It is packed, but they picked the perfect name for their business. We got our food almost immediately. The food is very good. They have one employee who does nothing but clean. She is either sweeping the floor, cleaning tables, refilling the catsup dispensers, napkins, etc., or cleaning the counter holding these things. The place is spotless.

With another wonderful and busy day behind us, we head to the hotel and call it a day.

Day Fifteen

Denise's parents, Harold and Lorraine, along with Lorraine's mother, Edith, are now here. Edith is lovingly known to my family as Granny. She is ninety-six years old and 5 feet tall at the most. She has one of the most beautiful smiles, and her eyes just sparkle with joy. Everyone is a little concerned about her handling the flight across the country, the sightseeing they are trying to do, and the wedding festivities because she does have a few health issues, but she is doing beautifully. Denise's sister, Catherine is here with her husband, David, and her brother, Brad is here with his son, Noah. Today, they are getting the tours we had earlier this week, so we are on our own.

We want to go back to Bodega Bay for more pictures. There is a huge boulder in the ocean with a very large hole in it. It almost looks like a tunnel.

I am still in awe of how hard the wind blows on the Pacific Coast compared with the ocean breeze on the Atlantic Coast. In the mornings, a jacket or sweatshirt feels good, even back inland as far as Santa Rosa. By lunch, short sleeves are comfortable, and at night, the jackets and sweatshirts need to be pulled back out.

Lunch was so good yesterday at Ike's. We are going back there, today.

We are spending the afternoon riding around and just taking pictures and enjoying the scenery. This area is so pretty, and the atmosphere is so relaxing.

After another really good meal at Black Bear Diner, we are heading back to the hotel to just relax and do nothing.

Day Sixteen

Enough of the sightseeing for now. We are here for a wedding, and it is time to give all our attention to that.

Andrew's brother, Adam, and his fiancée, Esther, are here. Adam is to be Andrew's best man, and Esther is to be a bridesmaid. Jay and Denise will have a busy (and expensive) summer of 2015. After Andrew and Chantel's June wedding, Jay and Denise will immediately go into planning mode for Adam and Esther's August wedding.

The rehearsal is this morning and will be followed by a Rehearsal Luncheon. Andrew wants two things for the Rehearsal Luncheon. One, he wants it to be completely laid-back and relaxing - nothing formal. Two, he wants the menu to have Short Sugar's barbecue from Reidsville, North Carolina. Jay and Denise met with David, the manager of Short Sugar's, who helped them decide how much barbecue would be needed for the number of people coming. This amount was frozen and shipped overnight to California.

Not only did Richard and Janelle invite Jay and Denise to stay with them during this time, but they also opened their kitchen for Denise to make the slaw, southern sweet tea and all the other fixings for the Rehearsal Luncheon so it could be as much like the east coast barbecue as possible.

Janelle got permission from her church to use their kitchen and outdoor area, which includes a covered picnic shelter. Jay, Denise, Richard and Janelle brought all the food over before going to the rehearsal. Phil and I are skipping the rehearsal and going to the church where someone will meet us and let us in. We are doing preliminary work until Jay and Denise get here. Then, we will all get in high gear to serve East Coast Barbecue and Southern Sweet Tea to a mostly West Coast group of people. It is a success.

The wedding party can relax in a very informal atmosphere and just enjoy themselves.

Richard and Janelle have been so gracious to help with so much for the Rehearsal Luncheon, it is only fair to help them. As soon as we cleaned up from the luncheon, the kitchen is immediately set up for mass production. Following the instructions, assembly lines are set up, and we begin making hors d'oeuvres for the wedding reception. Even some of the wedding party has come in to help on the assembly line. It is really turning work into a fun activity, with a lot of lively conversation.

Once all of that is completed, we clean up the kitchen, and everyone leaves to get ready for the big day tomorrow.

Day Seventeen

The big day is here. The wedding is at the Villa Chanticleer in Healdsburg, California. Perched on Fitch Mountain, it is a Wine Country wedding venue with magnificent views of Northern California's famous wine country and redwood groves. It is going to be an outdoor wedding in the Villa Gardens, and the weather is perfect.

The guests are being seated. It is time for the grandparents to be seated, and Andrew steps out of his role as groom and escorts his ninety-six years old great-grandmother down the aisle. Granny looks beautiful and is smiling that precious smile of hers. I am sure she is so proud that Andrew is honoring her in such a sweet and thoughtful way.

Andrew and the pastor appear in the gazebo at the front, and the procession begins. The bridesmaids are dressed in navy blue with navy blue flats. They are carrying a bouquet of white flowers. The groomsmen are dressed in tan slacks, a light blue shirt, navy blue suspenders, and navy blue tie. There are four young boys (I am guessing between the ages of five and seven) dressed in navy blue long pants, a white shirt, tan suspenders, a tan bow tie, and a tan beret. One of them is carrying a small wooden sign that looks to be about eighteen inches square, and something white is painted on it. As they come down the aisle, two go to stand with the bridesmaids, and two go to stand with the groomsmen. The maid of honor is dressed the same as the bridesmaids and is proceeding down the aisle to join them. The flower girl is dressed in white and looks precious as she also joins the bridesmaids. You can see the smile on Andrew's face, and you know Chantel has appeared. At that time, the young boy carrying the sign turns it around to the guests so they can read HERE COMES THE BRIDE. Chantel is so beautiful, as she walks down the aisle on the arm of Richard, in her white strapless wedding gown and carrying a bouquet of mostly white flowers with just a hint of pink mixed in. As she continues down the aisle, Andrew covers his eyes with his hands as tears of joy seem to erupt. His love for her is so evident.

Since I am on the front row, I am thinking everyone is looking at the bride and groom (and I want to have a few pictures to text home as soon as the wedding is over). I sneak out my cell phone, hold it low, and start snapping pictures.

"I now pronounce you man and wife" - The groom kisses the bride, and the married couple are introduced to the guests. What a beautiful and happy couple to watch walking up the aisle.

The reception is also held at Villa Chanticleer, but inside. There is a long table for the wedding party and a long table for the parents and grandparents. The rest of the banquet room is filled with tables for the guests. To mark our seats at the table for the parents and grandparents, there are slices of wood about one-half inch thick and about two inches in diameter sawed from a tree limb with our name written in black. I don't know if these were from a redwood tree or not, but we are bringing ours home to keep as a remembrance of the beautiful wedding.

The festivities are over, and we are heading back to our hotel to start packing for our return trip.

Expenses for Days Thirteen through Seventeen
>   Hotel   1,186.94
>   Food   238.24
>   Gas   29.00
>   Total   1,454.18

Gas is $3.299 per gallon at COSTCO in Rohnert Park, California on June 3, 2015.

Day Eighteen

It is 8:45 am. We are packed and are going to fill up the gas tank at COSTCO, while we have cheaper prices, and start our return trip home.

We missed San Francisco on the way to the wedding, so we are going to backtrack the roughly fifty-five miles and tour the city.

We can see the cloud as we approach. We have perfectly clear conditions and can see the fog at the top of the Golden Gate Bridge. As we approach, it is like riding under a cloud that is no more than ten feet above us. When we start coming off the bridge, it is completely clear again.

Have you heard about their tollbooths? Well, we were told that you just drive on through, the camera takes a picture of your license plate, and they will send you a bill in the mail. When we returned, we did receive a bill for $7.00 and paid it. All is good on that account. I am glad we had that bit of information.

We are heading to Fisherman's Wharf. Before we get out of the car, I want to text Denise. She, Jay, Adam and Esther are flying back together, and their flight is leaving much later today, so they are going to tour San Francisco, as well. If we are all here at the same time, we will see them one more time before we all go our separate ways. She says they are just getting ready to leave Santa Rosa.

We have checked out a little bit of Fisherman's Wharf and decide to walk the few blocks to Pier 39. A friend back home says this is a "must see". It really looks interesting with a lot of different gift shops and a lot of restaurants. As we start to walk under a wooden walkway with benches, we see a sign overhead on the walkway "End of Pier - BUBBA GUMP SHRIMP CO." We both love the 1994 film, "Forrest Gump." We are heading to Bubba Gump Shrimp Co. for lunch. I am getting the small order of Mama Blue's Southern Charmed Fried Shrimp with crispy fries and cocktail sauce. The cost is $15.99. It is delicious, the prices are reasonable for the area, and the view of San Francisco Bay is fantastic.

Walking back to see more of the shops and attractions on Pier 39, we hear the oddest noise, and it keeps getting louder. There is a large crowd on one side of the pier looking down into the water. Of course, we want to check it out. There are about twenty floating piers in the water. Sea lions are piled on top of most of the piers, and all seem to be making whatever type of noise sea lions make. What kind of noises do sea lions make? I think I can describe it as somewhere between a bark and a croak. Now, you know. Not only is the noise loud, but the smell is yucky. There is a sign advertising the Grand Opening of the Sea Lion Center on Pier 39. Although the noise is loud and the smell is yucky, we human beings are packed at the railing of the pier to watch them.

There is also an interesting sign entitled **The Big Quake**. It gives the history of how Pier 39 is built to withstand another 1909 style earthquake. The only problem, according to the sign, is The Embarcadero Roadway in front of Pier 39 is built on loosely packed landfill, which would liquefy like quicksand in a giant quake and turn Pier 39 into an island. The sign ends by saying "Thanks to the many fine restaurants and bars at Pier 39, you could have a great time here, even after the BIG ONE, while you are waiting for a rowboat to take you home."

I am a chocoholic, and I see the sign for Ghiradelli Square. Think Ginny - Ghirardelli means chocolate!! Phil and I have not been here long enough to learn about the streetcars and where you get on and off. I want to ride a streetcar up the hill to Ghirardelli Square, but we are afraid we may get on the wrong one and never return for a week, so we decide to walk. That little hill goes up and up, for blocks and blocks. We get almost there, and I decide not even the best chocolate is worth one more step up that hill. We turn around at Hyde Street Pier and slow down for about a minute. At least, the walk back is all downhill.

We make it back as far as Fisherman's Wharf and remember seeing a Jack-in-the-Box when we first parked. We are hot, tired, and ready for something to drink with a lot of ice, and I want to sit for a minute and text Denise to see if they are here yet. If not, we are hitting the road. I don't think an ice-cold drink ever tasted so good, or sitting down ever felt so good.

I text Denise, and they have just gotten to Pier 39. After resting for a few minutes, and refilling drinks to carry with us, we walk the few blocks back to see them. We all watch the smelly, loud sea lions, and walk around for a while, looking in the shops. Now, it is time to give hugs and wish everyone a safe trip home. We walk back to our car and begin our return trip. I don't know if I have ever walked this many miles in any one day of my life, especially the uphill ones. I am really looking forward to just sitting in the car for a while.

We are leaving San Francisco by way of the Bay Bridge, which will put us on the next part of our trip. It has a tollbooth like the Golden Gate Bridge. Well, maybe not exactly like the Golden Gate Bridge. Little do we know that a few weeks after we return home, we will receive in the mail **a Notice of Toll Evasion**. The toll amount is $5.00, the toll evasion penalty is $25.00 for a total amount of $30.00. At the bottom of the notice, it says "Failure to respond to this notice may result in additional penalties and fees and referral of the amount due to a collections agency and/or withholding of your vehicle registration". My first thought is this is not good. Thirty dollars is a lot of money to pay for stupidity. So, I wrote a letter -

Dear Sirs,

We are in our seventies and have never been west of the Mississippi and decided to take a cross-country tour.

In our state of North Carolina, we just go through the toll, they take a picture of our license plate, and they bill us, like the Golden Gate Bridge.

We honestly thought FASTRAK was the same way. We would have never gone through it if we had known you are supposed to stop and pay.

I am enclosing a check for $5.00 in hopes that you will be understanding of our lack of knowledge of FASTRAK.

If you feel you must penalize us for our ignorance, please send us a bill for the penalty and we will pay it.

Thank you for your consideration

Sincerely,

Evidently, they felt there are really people who are not up to date on how some toll fees are handled. They accepted our check, and I really appreciate their kindness.

Now that we are continuing our trip, we just called for reservations for tonight in Fairfield, California. Phil has a friend from his high school days, who is also a friend of his family, and lives in Dixon, which is right at Fairfield. He wants to give him a call. Whenever Ned comes to North Carolina, he always goes to see Phil's mom and his sisters, Margie and

Ginger. They will usually call Phil to come join them, or Ned will come to see us.

After checking into the hotel, Phil calls Ned. He is coming to the hotel, and we are all going out to dinner. There is a Panera Bread adjacent to the hotel and we are going there.

We had a very nice visit with Ned and are so glad we planned this into our trip.

We are staying tonight at Hilton Garden Inn in Fairfield, California.

Expenses for Day Eighteen   Hotel   202.27
                             Food   96.19
                             Gas   35.00
                             Total   333.46

Gas is $3.259 per gallon at COSTCO in Rohnert, California on June 8, 2015.

Day Nineteen

As we leave Fairfield, we notice the mountains are again brown, the trees are larger, and the hillside is breathtaking. Red, pink, and white flowers are on bushes planted in the median from Fairfield for at least twenty miles.

Eighty-five miles southwest of Reno, the landscape is changing to pines.

There are signs on the highway for "chain service" and "watch out for snow removal equipment." My ears are popping. Signs are showing 3,000 and 5,000 ft. elevation. We are beginning to see rocks again. The sides of the mountains are rocks and less trees. There are wide pull-off lanes with signs that read "chain installation only." We are into serious snow country.

We are taking the exit from the interstate to go to the northern end of Lake Tahoe. It is beautiful. There is no swimming allowed where we are, but there are plenty of boats and kayaks. Even at the end of the pier, you can see the bottom of the lake. We can see a lot of rocks, broken pieces of wood, fish and a snake. I have just seen the first snake of our trip, and I am so glad it is in the water. The snake looks to be about eighteen inches long, about the size of my index finger, and black and yellow stripes run from its head to its tail. It is swimming with the fish, and it does not seem to bother them, so, evidently, they are not his food. Bicycles are everywhere. Phil is talking to one biker who says there is a 170 miles long path that goes around the entire lake.

On the way to Lake Tahoe, we noticed a sign to Squaw Valley, so we decided we would go there as we left the lake. There are signs with the Olympic torch under them as we approach the entrance to Olympic Village. There are shops, hotels, and restaurants in a very relaxed setting, and the gondolas taking skiers to the top of the mountain are very impressive.

Two very interesting and informative side trips.

We are going through Reno to see the sights, and then we will spend the night in a more relaxed atmosphere on the outskirts of Reno.

Tonight, we are staying at a Hampton Inn in Reno, Nevada.

Our expenses for Day Nineteen
Hotel	159.95	
Food	43.36	
Gas	40.00	
Total		243.31

Gas is $3.899 per gallon In Lake Tahoe, California on June 9, 2015.

Day Twenty

 Today is a day of driving, with no tourist attractions along the way. We are leaving Reno and heading to Salt Lake City on highway I-80.

 The scenery is flat. No houses. No businesses. Nothing. We are just driving to make miles. The highway is excellent, and you can see for miles. The one thing that catches my eye is the dual lane roads do not have medians between them. How do you cross to turn around and go back? We can see the other lane, but it looks to be about a tenth of a mile away, with no roads to connect the two. I keep thinking. If an emergency vehicle comes one way, how does the driver go back? Then, I decide they probably all have four-wheel drives, so they can just drive across the land to get to the other lane. I am thinking. With a dual lane road on perfectly flat land, and no roads coming into it, the chances of an accident are very small. Probably, the only time an emergency vehicle would be needed would be for a medical emergency.

 I guess God wants us to have a little excitement in our otherwise boring drive, because Phil notices our VSA light on the Honda has come on, and we no longer have cruise control. We are in the middle of nowhere. He tells me to get out the maintenance manual and read. Phil is very smart when it comes to understanding how a car works. I know nothing. From the questions he is asking me, and the answers I give him from the manual, he decides we are low on transmission fluid. He pulls over to check, and we are. The manual says we are to only use Honda transmission fluid. If we cannot get Honda fluid, there is one other kind we can use, but we are to take it to a Honda dealership as soon as possible and have that flushed out and replaced with Honda fluid. One question is, "Can we add the second-choice fluid and use it for the rest of our trip, or do we need to stop at the nearest Honda dealership and have it flushed and replaced?" The nearest dealership is in Salt Lake City, which is over 300 miles away. Phil taught me to keep all maintenance records in the glove compartment, so I get one of the receipts from our local dealership and find the phone number. The service manager tells me we will be okay to use the second choice of fluid for the remainder of the trip, but to come to see them as soon as we get back, so they can flush and replace. Now, we need to find a store that sells the fluid we need. We finally do, and Phil adds the fluid. Everything is fine. We do have AAA as a backup, if we need to be towed, but thanks to Phil, that is not necessary.

Tonight, we are staying in Elko, Nevada. One of the first things I notice, as we enter the town, is a huge letter E painted in white on the side of a mountain. I question one of the locals as to why they have this, and she says it is to show the significance of their town. I have noticed a lot of the towns in this part of our trip will also paint the first letter of the town on a mountain. I am thinking. This could be helpful to pilots flying overhead, in identifying the town over which they are flying. Since these letters have lights shining on them to make them visible at night, that should be a pretty sight from an airplane.

    We are staying tonight at a Hilton Garden Inn in Elko, Nevada.

Expenses for Day Twenty are Hotel   153.44
                             Food   31.69
                             Gas   19.00
                             Total   204.13

Gas is $2.999 per gallon in Lovelock, Nevada on June 10, 2015.

Day Twenty-One

It is another beautiful day for traveling, and we are heading to Salt Lake City. We are still in Nevada, and have a lot of driving before there are more tourist attractions. There are more windmill farms visible as we continue. I guess the wind can pick up speed across this flat land and make those blades move rather fast.

Phil is looking for Bonneville Salt Flats. According to Wikipedia, "The Bonneville Salt Flats is a densely packed salt pan in Tooele County in northwestern Utah. The area is a remnant of the Pleistocene Lake Bonneville and is the largest of many salt flats located west of the Great Salt Lake." This is a place people go to set land speed records on all types of motor vehicles. Since the area is 40 square miles, they have plenty of distance to build up their speed, and to slow down. The compressed salt gives it a hard driving surface. Just as Phil is voicing his concern that there have been no signs for this, we spot a small sign that shows Bonneville Salt Flats to the left. We turn and go about a half mile to the end of the road and turn right to go to where some cars are parked, and people are walking around. There are no cars driving on the salt flats, and we notice the flats are covered with water. One of the signs they have states that speed trials are scheduled throughout the summer and fall. They end when rain covers the area with water. We are told we missed the time trials by about two weeks. In every other body of water where we stopped, we have taken off shoes and gotten a picture of us with our feet in the water. We are doing it here, as well.

Leaving Bonneville, we now head to the Great Salt Lake. All along the road are big patches of salt like the salt flats, and then, the windmill farms start up again. It is an interesting and different type of scenery than we have seen before. There is the sign for The Great Salt Lake and Marina. As we step out of the car, the smell is awful. There are pleasure boats on the lake, and people are walking into the water. I am heading down to get my picture made putting my feet into the water. Phil says with the smell, he is going to skip this one, and I can put my feet in for both of us. The closer we get, the worse the smell becomes. By the time we reach the edge of the water, I notice there are little flying insects everywhere - sitting on top of the water, and flying right above the water. They are so thick that it almost looks like a solid brown and black cloud, and the smell is even worse at the water than when we got out of the car. I can't do it. I just cannot put my feet through all those insects, just to say I put my feet in the Great Salt Lake. We have seen what we wanted to see, and now we are leaving.

The closer we get to Salt Lake City, the more congested the traffic is becoming. We are now approaching a sign warning of a detour ahead, for the highway on which we are traveling. We are getting a little stressed, because we are supposed to turn within a few miles, and we do not know if this detour will bring us out before, or after, our turn. Phil is asking where he should go, while he is still driving closer to the detour. In panic mode, I am reaching for the map. My cell phone rings. Our friend, Mac does not text, but he calls every day or so, to see where we are, and how things are going. Mac is calling. I quickly answer the phone with, "Hi, Mac." "Can I call you back in a few minutes?" Thankfully, he does not ask any questions, and says that will be fine. We are pulling into a convenience store parking lot, and evaluating the situation. We find our own detour that will keep us on our route, and we are happy. We are now returning Mac's call.

When we requested a route from AAA, they not only sent us three maps - one each for Eastern states, Central states and Western states, but they also sent three books to go with each map written out according to miles. Example: go 3 miles, turn left on such and such street and go 7 miles, etc. We notice the book is taking us right into the center of Salt Lake City. We question their decision and decide to take the bypass around the city to avoid the heavy traffic. We will learn later that the Mormon Tabernacle is located in the center of Salt Lake City. Our mistake.

Since our next big tourist attraction is Yellowstone National Park, we are heading that way.

We are staying tonight at a Hampton Inn in Logan, Utah.

Bonneville Salt Flats Under Water

Expenses for Day Twenty-One   Hotel   142.67
                                                Food   24.68
                                                Gas   53.02
                                                Total   220.37

Gas is $3.099 per gallon in Elko, Nevada on June 11, 2015. Gas is $2.999 per gallon in Bountiful, Utah on June 11, 2015.

Day Twenty-Two

As we leave Logan, Utah, and go into Idaho, I notice the scenery. It reminds me of West Virginia, or at least the part we are going through.

We are heading to Yellowstone, and the last stop before that is Jackson Hole, Wyoming. We are calling ahead for reservations, and learn that because this is the last stop before Yellowstone if you are coming from the south, the hotel rooms are extremely expensive.

I thought Jackson Hole was the name of the town, but upon researching this, I have learned that Jackson Hole is the name of the valley in which Jackson sits, along with several other towns.

We are going through Afton, Wyoming, and notice an arch over the street made of elk horns. On top of the arch are two stuffed elk who are locking horns. There is a sign with the arch that states, **"World's Largest Elkhorn Arch."**

As we enter Jackson, I am in awe. I feel as though I have just stepped back in time to the cowboy days. Everything is western. There is a Town Square, and on each corner, there is an Elk Antler Arch. We are walking around in the middle of town and going into the different shops when we spot Wort

Hotel Silver Dollar Bar & Grill. The name just sounds western, and we want to check this out. The food is delicious, and the atmosphere puts us back to the cowboy days. I love it.

One thing I notice is they have real cowboys here. There are rodeos and advertisements for championship rodeos everywhere. In our hotel, I notice two young girls, probably college age, and I tell Phil that they are real cowgirls. He asks me how I know, and I tell him because they are wearing spurs.

We are staying tonight at a Hampton Inn in Jackson, Wyoming.

World's Largest Elkhorn Arch

Expenses for Day Twenty-Two   Hotel   322.92
                              Food   38.47
                              Gas   13.00
                              Total   374.39

Gas is $2.999 per gallon in Logan, Utah on June 12, 2015.

Day Twenty-Three

    I really hate to leave Jackson. I fell in love with its beauty and western atmosphere, but this is the day to head north.

    We reach Grand Teton National Park, and they have a $30.00 admission fee, which our Senior Lifetime Pass covers. Although it is June, the mountain peaks are still covered with snow. We stay in our cars, drive through, and pull off whenever we want a picture or a better view. A man is pulling over to the side of the road and taking a drone out of the trunk of his car. We decide to stop and see what he is going to do. He is sending the drone up and guiding it to the backside of the mountains. We assume he has a camera on the drone and is getting some pretty good pictures.

    As we go further, there is a sign that states **"Old Faithful - 17 Miles."** We go further, and there is a sign letting us know we are crossing the Continental Divide with an elevation of 8,391 feet.

    Now, for Yellowstone National Park. Admission is also $30.00 and once again, we use our Senior Lifetime Pass. Everyone drives their cars through the park and can get out at all the special scenic pull-offs, or only the ones they want to see. I feel better being in the car since the wild animals roam free throughout the park. There is a breathtaking waterfall, called Kepler Cascades, that reminds me again of the great masterpiece God has painted of the earth, just for our enjoyment.

Old Faithful is one of the attractions I really want to see, and we are here. There are several rows of wooden benches placed around in a circular shape, covering about one fourth of the distance around the circle, and people are sitting here waiting for the next eruption. We were told it is not the biggest or the most regular geyser in Yellowstone. There are a lot of geysers in the park, but this is the most popular because it is the biggest regular geyser. A lot of hot springs are visible throughout the park, and they are roped off with warnings of the extremely hot water.

As we continue to ride along, we see a lot of areas where it is evident there has been a large forest fire, and we notice some of the most beautiful wildflowers I have ever seen. We discuss how disappointed we are that we have not seen any wildlife, and we are on our way out. Then, about thirty feet to the right of the car, there is an elk. All cars are pulling over to watch the beautiful animal as he grazes in the wilds. He stops eating, looks up at all the cars, and with an, "Oh, well," expression, he continues his grazing. I guess we humans and our cars are so common to him, he feels no danger and is completely at home.

We have thoroughly enjoyed our day at these two national parks, and it is now time to take the east exit and head for

Cody, Wyoming. All along the road, we can see small hot springs erupting in the fields and by the highway.

Cody still has the western theme throughout. The Irma Hotel, Restaurant, and Saloon was built by Buffalo Bill in 1902. We know this is where we want to eat tonight. The food is good. There is a Buffalo Bill impersonator walking around talking to the customers as they eat, and I am expecting to see either Annie Oakley, or a gun-slinging cowboy come in just any minute. I think I could quickly adapt to this western culture.

We are staying tonight at a Comfort Inn in Cody, Wyoming.

Old Faithful

Kepler Cascades in Yellowstone National Park

Expenses for Day Twenty-Three Hotel   192.24
                               Food   47.94
                               Gas   23.01
                               Total   263.19

Gas is $2.899 per gallon in Jackson Hole, Wyoming on June 13, 2015.

Day Twenty-Four

Today, we are leaving Cody, Wyoming, and heading southeast, with all our next tourist destinations being in South Dakota, so this will be a mileage day only. After such a full day yesterday, it is rather nice just to ride and see the countryside.

We notice the land is changing from so many mountains to more flat plains, and the wind is getting stronger, which means we are also seeing more windmill farms.

The ride is also giving me time to reflect on the Wild West atmosphere we have experienced the last few days. I know we only went through the northern part of Texas, but Wyoming felt more like cowboy territory than the parts of Texas through which we traveled. We have friends back home who go to Wyoming on hunting trips. They are always talking about how much they like Jackson Hole and how pretty the scenery is there. I can completely understand their love of this wonderful part of our nation.

The wind is really picking up, and it is time to stop at a rest stop for lunch. Do you remember those rest stops in the southwest with three sides to them to knock off the wind? Well, these have two sides. Evidently, they know which way the wind will blow all the time and have placed them strategically to block that wind.

We are staying tonight at a Hampton Inn in Casper, Wyoming.

Windmill Farm in Wyoming

Expenses for the Day Twenty-Four Hotel   184.21
                                   Food   15.09
                                   Gas   24.00
                                   Total   223.30

Gas is $2.799 per gallon in Cody, Wyoming on June 14, 2015.

Day Twenty-Five

Our first stop of the day is Crazy Horse Memorial. We are going to a short video/lecture explaining the history of this memorial.

Is seems that sculptor Korczak Ziolkowski received a letter from Lakota Chief Henry Standing Bear inviting him to come to the Black Hills of South Dakota and carve a mountain. Mr. Kiolkowski had worked at Mount Rushmore as an assistant in 1939. Chief Henry Standing Bear, and other leaders, chose the Sioux Warrior Crazy Horse as the subject. Crazy Horse was born in the Black Hills and is partially credited with Custer's defeat at the Battle of Little Bighorn. Construction began in 1948. Depicting Crazy Horse atop his steed, the 563-foot-tall memorial is supposed to dwarf even the four presidents on Mount Rushmore when completed.

After the death of Mr. Kiolkowski, his wife and family attempted to complete this work. Mrs. Kiolkowski died in 2014. To date, six of the Ziolkowski children and some grandchildren are carrying on the family legacy at Crazy Horse.

One of the things stressed in the video is Crazy Horse Memorial is <u>not</u> a federal or state project. They accept no money from the United States Government. It is financed primarily from an admission fee. The admission fee is $11.00 per person. The mission of the memorial is to preserve the culture, tradition, and living heritage of the North American Indians. I learned so much from this visit.

After a drive of about ten miles, we are now at Mount Rushmore.

Danish-American sculptor, Gutzon Borglum, his son, Lincoln, and over four hundred workers, sculpted out of granite in the Black Hills, four presidents representing the first one hundred and fifty years of American history. Those presidents are George Washington, Thomas Jefferson, Theodore Roosevelt and Abraham Lincoln.

It is impressive, and it is history, but Phil and I were both expecting it to be much larger than it is.

We are now passing through Custer, South Dakota, and notice a restaurant with benches in front and a line of people waiting to get in. Normally, we will not wait in a long line at a restaurant, but this place must have great food, so we are going to stop and check it out. While waiting in line, we tell another man, also in line, that this is our first time here. He tells Phil that we will see that the food is well worth the wait. Now that we are in and looking at the menu, Phil decides on a cheeseburger. I am going to live dangerously and have my first buffalo burger. The buffalo burger has a different taste, but it is not bad. Phil says his cheeseburger is the best he has ever had and wants me to take a bite - very, very delicious. Little do we know that several months later, we hear on television that burgers from Black Hills Burger and Bun Co. in Custer, South Dakota were voted "Best Burger in the Country." Just think, Ginny. You could have had the best burger in the country, but you chose a "not bad" buffalo burger, instead. Not a wise choice on your part. At least, Phil gave me a bite of his.

We are staying tonight at a Baymont Inn & Suites in Rapid City, South Dakota.

Expenses for Day Twenty-Five   Hotel   196.22
                                Food   42.49
                                Gas   45.00
                                Total   283.71

Gas is $2.599 per gallon in Casper, Wyoming on June 15, 2015.

Gas is $2.559 per gallon in Custer, South Dakota on June 15, 2015.

Day Twenty-Six

As we are leaving our hotel in Rapid City, I tell the young lady at the desk we are heading to the Badlands, and she asks me if we are going to stop at Wall Drug. I tell her I have never heard of Wall Drug. She describes it briefly, and I know we need to add this to our stops.

Wall Drug is another world. The story goes that in 1931, Ted and Dorothy Hustead bought the only drug store in Wall. By the summer of 1936, the business had not grown much and one Sunday Dorothy noticed there were still a lot of cars going by on the hot, dusty prairie road and came up with an idea to offer free ice water. Once the sign was up, the business started to increase and grew from there. Wall Drug is now an entire block, with individual tourist-type stores under one roof. They have stores for mining, a rock shop, chapel, boots and western wear, camera and film, hunting supplies, a lot of eating facilities, gift shops, and much more. Moreover, they still offer free ice water.

The Badlands is our next stop. We are driving through and see bighorn sheep everywhere. As we pull over to take pictures, a mother sheep and her little ones are walking up a narrow rock formation, which is right at us, but they don't seem to be concerned with all the cars and humans around. As we continue our drive, the vistas become more awesome. I feel like I am back at the Grand Canyon, except with the Grand Canyon, I looked down and out. Here, I am looking down and up and out at the prairie.

All through our trip, we have seen signs, "**Beware of Poisonous Snakes**," but here, they are more specific "**Beware Rattlesnakes**." We are pulling in a parking lot where we can get out and walk to an area to take pictures. One of these signs is right by the walkway, which has tall grass on both sides. Phil is getting out to walk up that walkway to take pictures. I am staying in the car to avoid the rattlesnakes. While I am waiting, two employees are walking down the walk holding long poles with a sharp point on the end. They are stabbing the poles into the tall grass. I am sure they are looking for rattlesnakes or trying to kill them where they are. Thank goodness, no snakes are coming out while they are stabbing. Enough reason for me to stay in the car.

I have always heard of the Badlands of South Dakota, but I never realized they would be this beautiful. One more example of God's masterpiece of the earth He created, just for our enjoyment.

There is a gift shop on the right as we are leaving. We decide to stop. The pottery they have is beautiful. We decide which piece we want to purchase, and we are surprised and happy to learn that the pottery comes with a certificate of authenticity. It was designed and handcrafted by a Sioux

Indian artist and was made from the red clay of the Black Hills (Paha Sapa), sacred to the Lakota people, and a fine white clay from Kentucky. It is designed, handcrafted, and decorated with designs and symbols important to their culture. On the back of the certificate of authenticity is a list of the Sioux Symbols and Designs and what each one means. I fell in love with the Badlands, and I now have a beautiful piece of local pottery, and I also have some red clay from the Badlands.

We are leaving the Badlands and are heading home. There is just one more tourist attraction in Indiana on our list. But then, we never know what will be around the next turn. As we are driving along the highway, we notice a sign for 1880 Town. Not wanting to miss anything, we pull in. The first thing we see is a wooden sign that states, "1880 Town, Dakota Territory, Elevation 2391 Ft., Population: 170 Ghosts, 9 Cats, 3 Dogs, 2 Rabbits, which has been crossed out from 2 to 9, which has been crossed out from 9 to 36, which has been crossed out from 36 to 870, which has been crossed out to a total of 3,905 Rabbits."

The town has more than thirty buildings from the 1880 to 1920 era, which are furnished with relics, historical accounts and photographs. Among some of the buildings is a fire company, hotel, emporium, church, saddle shop, homes, and a Wells Fargo Station with its stagecoach in front. It is so interesting going back in history and seeing how they lived during those years.

We are staying tonight at a Hampton Inn in Mitchell, South Dakota.

South Dakota Badlands

Expenses for Day Twenty-Six Hotel   141.12
                             Food   13.35
                             Gas   42.00
                             Total   196.47

Gas is $2.869 per gallon in Kadoka, South Dakota on June 16, 2015.

Gas is $2.779 per gallon in Mitchell, South Dakota on June 16, 2015.

Day Twenty-Seven

With no more tourist attractions at this point, we are making miles. We are still seeing a lot of windmill farms and beautiful scenery, but we have been away from home for twenty-six days. Phil is getting homesick for his Model T Fords, and I am homesick for my sons, daughters-in-law, and grandchildren. We are heading home.

We are staying tonight at a Hampton Inn in Moline, Illinois.

Expenses for Day Twenty-Seven Hotel   151.54
                                Food   43.63
                                Gas   27.00
                                Total   222.17

Gas is $2.559 per gallon in Clear Lake, Iowa on June 17, 2015.

Day Twenty-Eight

We are moving right along on our trip home. We have one more stop to make, and then we will have seen everything we have on our list of things we wanted to see and places we wanted to go.

In 2008, they celebrated the 100th anniversary of the Model T Ford in Indiana. Phil had just finished restoring his 1916 Model T Depot Hack. He was going to trailer it up there and participate in the tour of cars they had planned as part of the celebration. They were also going to the Model T Museum in Richmond, Indiana. He had been looking forward to this for about a year, and reservations had been made. I had some health issues pop up that required me to have surgery as soon as possible. The earliest the surgeon could schedule it was the same week as the 100th anniversary celebration. I wanted to hold off, but Phil wanted to cancel our trip and schedule my surgery, which we did. I am fine now, but I have always felt guilty that he missed something he had been looking forward to for so long.

Our last stop on the way home is Richmond, Indiana. I owe him big-time, and he can spend as much time in the museum as he wants.

We are staying tonight at a Hampton Inn in Richmond, Indiana.

Expenses for Day Twenty-Eight Hotel 147.89
Food 15.38
Gas 57.00
Total 220.27

Gas is $2.799 per gallon in Moline, Illinois on June 18, 2015.

Gas is $2.799 per gallon in Brownsburg, Indiana on June 18, 2015.

Day Twenty-Nine

The Model T Museum doesn't open until 10:00 am, and we are having a lazy morning. At 10:00 am sharp, we head through the doors, and Phil takes it all in and asks the curator a lot of questions. I do not think he is missing a single item, but I do think he is enjoying every minute. After a few hours, he is ready to leave.

It is 492 miles from Richmond to Reidsville and it is a little after 12:00 noon. After a short discussion, we both agree that we want to sleep in our own bed tonight. I text Kris and Jay, and tell them I will not be texting later to give the name of a hotel, because we are coming home. It will be late, but we will be home.

We are exhausted from today's long ride, but we are home, and for the rest of our lives, we can enjoy the memories of our Trip of a Lifetime.

We are staying tonight at our home, in our bed.

Expenses for Day Twenty-Nine   Food   20.31
Gas   54.00
Total   74.31

Gas is $2.799 per gallon in Rio Grande, Ohio on June 19, 2015.

Gas is $2.499 per gallon in Fancy Gap, Virginia on June 19, 2015.

Was It Worth It?

Total Days	29
Total Mileage	7,695 MILES
Total Hotel Expense	$4,998.42
Total Food Expense	$1,133.38
Total Gas Expense	$ 854.22
Total Expenses	$6,986.02
Money Saved Through Senior Lifetime Pass	$120.00

We would do it again in a heartbeat, or using the ideas we put in place for this trip, we would embark on another trip to somewhere else we haven't been. Who knows? We may run across another Petrified Forest, or Wall Drug, or Squaw Valley, or 1880 Town. It's the unexpected surprises that just pop up that makes this kind of trip so special.

Dear Reader,

Just writing this book and reliving all the things we did, the places we saw, and the experiences we encountered, makes me thirsty to start planning another trip.

I hope reading the book makes you thirsty, too, to start planning Your Own Trip of a Lifetime.

Tornado Alley

Road Condition Phone Numbers
May 23, 2015

Arkansas	800-245-1672
Colorado	303-639-1111
Kansas	866-511-5368
Missouri	800-222-6400
New Mexico	800-432-4269
Oklahoma	888-425-2385
Texas	800-452-9292

Senior Lifetime Pass Changes

On August 28, 2017, the price of the Senior Lifetime Pass increased to $80.00. This pass is a one-time fee for U.S. citizens or permanent residents age 62 or over. It may be obtained in person at a federal recreation site, most national parks, or through the mail using the application form and paying an additional $10.00 handling fee.

There is also a $20.00 annual senior pass, which is good for just one year.

These passes admit owner of pass and passengers in a regular passenger car when charge is by the car. If charge is per person, the pass will cover owner and three other adults (no more than four total), (children under sixteen are always free).

There are a lot of other discounts covered under these passes at federal recreation sites (such as camping, swimming, boat launching, and guided tours).

I am sure you can call any federal national park or federal recreation site for more information.

Oh, if you lose your pass, they will not replace it. You must get a new one.

Your Notes for Your Trip of a Lifetime